FROM
ESSENCE
TO
EXPRESSION

HOW TO CREATE A BRAND
FROM NOTHING

ALEXANDER SANSON

AuthorHouse™
1663 Liberty Drive
Bloomington, IN 47403
www.authorhouse.com
Phone: 1-800-839-8640

© 2012 by Alexander Sanson. All rights reserved.

No part of this book may be reproduced, stored in a retrieval system, or transmitted by any means without the written permission of the author.

Published by AuthorHouse   12/05/2012

ISBN: 978-1-4772-4685-6 (sc)
ISBN: 978-1-4772-4684-9 (e)

Any people depicted in stock imagery provided by Thinkstock are models, and such images are being used for illustrative purposes only.
Certain stock imagery © Thinkstock.

This book is printed on acid-free paper.

Because of the dynamic nature of the Internet, any web addresses or links contained in this book may have changed since publication and may no longer be valid. The views expressed in this work are solely those of the author and do not necessarily reflect the views of the publisher, and the publisher hereby disclaims any responsibility for them.

Dedicated to my family

INTRODUCTION
9

CHAPTER 1
An overview of branding
15

CHAPTER 2
The value of branding
29

CHAPTER 3
What to brand, when to brand
53

CHAPTER 4
The all-important brand essence
65

CHAPTER 5
Eight steps to getting branded
97

FINAL THOUGHTS
129

BRAND ESSENCE EXERCISES
137

HEART-FELT THANKS AND
ABOUT THE AUTHOR
150

INTRODUCTION

INTRODUCTION

I have often wondered why I love branding so much. It's probably because I love business so much and for me, branding is synonymous with business development and growth.

My background is in graphic design and over the past ten years I have been honoured to help contribute to some of the greatest brands in the world including Rolls-Royce, Barclays, HSBC and adidas.

It was when I went independent and started working for smaller businesses to help them build their brands that I really started to see the value in my work.

Business owners come to me with nothing physical to show for their business and leave a month or two later with a tangible, credible, professional looking interface that positions them as a real entity, a player in the market place.

Before getting branded, customers, investors and partners would slip past them through the ether, but branding has given them a presence, a real-life surface for eyeballs to be drawn to.

My job is to bring my clients' businesses to life. It is rewarding to see them receive such tremendous energy boosts when they finally see in front of them what they

INTRODUCTION

have been struggling to express for so long.

Branding, as you will see, is more than just a paint job. When done properly, it is a highly introspective process for the business owner and demands rigor, honesty and commitment from all parties.

In social situations, I have met a lot of business people who tell me that they "might need help" with their logo or that they "really need to do something" about their website or "simply can't stand" their business cards. But I can quickly tell whether they'll be phoning the next day to ask for an exploratory meeting with regards to their branding.

The ones who get their diaries out on the spot are those who have linked not having a brand with their business suffering.

Those who disappear, never to be heard from again, still think that branding means changing the colours on their website.

Branding is not rocket science. Think of it as a bit of science and a bit of art mixed together under one roof. It is perfectly possible to create strong branding whatever your background and whatever your business as long as you know what you are looking for in the first place and

INTRODUCTION

---

understand the process required. In this book I want to achieve two things: teach you about what branding really is and give you the tools to get your branding well underway.

Let's get started!

CHAPTER 1
An overview of branding

WHAT IS A BRAND?

"A brand is a living entity – and it is enriched or undermined cumulatively over time, the product of a thousand small gestures."
– Michael Eisner, CEO Disney

A brand is the experience, or culmination of experiences, that you share with your customers.

More accurately, it is the interface between your organization and your valued audience, experienced through multiple touch-points (or "a thousand small gestures" to quote Eisner).

These touch-points (or gestures) include your logo, website, sales brochure and business card. But they go beyond mere "branded" objects. They are every single facet of your organization a person comes into contact with: a properly cleaned rest room; a smiling assistant; a well-conceived freebee at the shop counter; the smell of the office junior's deodorant (or lack thereof!) as he passes you in the corridor. All these touch-points add up to create the overall experience and hence your "brand".

> *"Products are made in the factory,
> but brands are created in the mind."*
> – Walter Landor, Landor Associates

Because a brand is an experience, by definition it takes place in our mind. It is therefore a personal experience. Different people carry around with them different "brands" or perceptions of your organization.

The most powerful and influential businesses (most of the household names we see around us) are those that create a **consistent** experience for their customers. They have mastered the art of systematically delivering positive associations and experiences to people who then share those experiences through word of mouth with the people who trust them.

It is this consistency that gives good brands traction in the market.

Consistency provides people with reference points to share their personal experiences with others. This builds collective experiences which create compounding effects for the brand and is why so many people have similar views about certain brands.

Michael E. Gerber, author of the E-Myth, explains that one of the most important things a business must do is deliver consistently to its customers. Gerber was talking specifically about products and services – a major aspect of the experience being created by the organization. Consistency is equally important for the rest of your brand's expression.

People revisit brands because they trust them to deliver a specific experience to a certain standard. Any kink in the consistency threatens to break this trust. In this respect, brands draw up unwritten contracts between businesses and customers.

> *"Your brand is created out of customer contact and the experience your customers have of you."*
> – Stelios Haji-Ioannou, Chairman, EasyGroup

Employees, their behaviour, demeanour, and energy are crucial contributors to your organization's brand. If we leave a store or office feeling good about the service, that brand is buoyed in our minds.

Your brand carries with it and communicates your organization's reputation, character, promise and essence. It represents the magical gap between a commodity that anyone can buy anywhere and the must-have product for which people pay extra.

Crucially, a brand creates value in the hearts and minds of customers.

ESSENCE AND EXPRESSION

Brand can be split into two distinct areas: essence and expression.

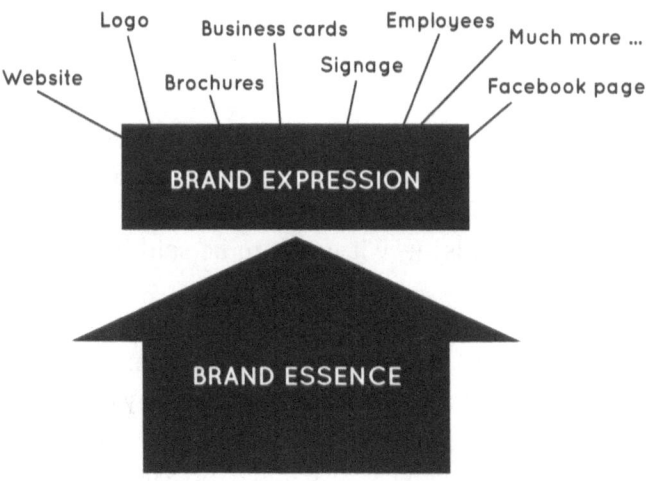

Brand essence is the philosophy that drives the organization. It's the intangible *idea*, crystallized into words, that works behind the scenes and acts as the spirit or soul of what you are building.

Brand expression is the means through which the brand's essence is expressed – those multiple touch points or gestures on the literal, sensory level. It is your logo, website, sales force, receptionist, business card and everything else that creates an experience for a person when they interact with your business. As you can tell from the illustration on the previous page, a lot of a brand's expression needs to be created by a graphic designer.

Essence guides expression. See brand expression as *how* something is said in a conversation. See brand essence as *what* is said and (in the case of the most powerful brands) *why* it needs to be said in the first place.

From Chapter 4 onwards this will be examined more thoroughly and will constitute one of the key messages in the book – you will see why I have made the distinction between essence and expression and why expression follows essence, not the other way around.

MARKETING AND GRAPHIC DESIGN

Marketing, the activity of promoting a business, is delivered through the various elements of the brand expression: typically brochures, gifts, sponsorship, Facebook, emails, tweets, websites, etc.

Marketing is part of the interface that creates the experience for the business's target market. I therefore consider it a subset of brand.

Graphic design constitutes a huge part of the brand expression and is needed to create most of the marketing collateral. A logo is considered graphic design. A website is considered graphic design. It's the same with brochures, business cards, posters, signage, etc. Often times these elements that have been created by a graphic designer are referred to as brand*ing*.

It is imperative for any business to have a graphic designer work with them to build their brand. With the right instructions, a well-trained graphic designer can create an interface (a logo, a website, a business card, whatever else is deemed necessary) within months, sometimes weeks. A graphic designer can mean the difference between you having no visual presence in the public's mind and you being able to own your territory in the market.

An overview of branding

DON'T CONFUSE LOGO WITH BRAND

Many business owners hunt down a graphic designer to create a logo, thinking it's the solution to their branding challenge. Whilst I consider a logo to be part of the brand*ing*, I would never refer to it as the business's *brand*. A logo is the tip of the iceberg. If communication stops at the logo, your business can quickly be perceived as insubstantial or even untrustworthy.

Let's look at the analogy of a home to show how the logo fits into the bigger branding picture:

Think of yourself as your business and your home as your brand. In many ways your home is an extension of yourself: it reflects your tastes, your living habits, your lifestyle.

Think of your logo as the front door to your brand.

The rest of your home: the building itself; the walls; electrics; plumbing; furnishings; wallpaper; the way the colour schemes work; etc; right down to the interior design minutiae, represents the rest of your brand.

The logo is just one (fairly important) aspect of your

brand. Having just a logo designed for your business is like having a front door to your home and nothing else.

CREATING THE EXPERIENCE

There are several reasons why I like the home analogy:

- The foundations of a home represent the brand essence, below the surface but integral to the structure and endurance of the building, while the rest of the building represents the brand expression.

- In the same way that brands line up on the high

street or on Google's pages, people can view your home from the outside and either be drawn towards it, pass by it with indifference, or feel repelled by it.

• You build a home one brick at a time. You build a brand one touch point at a time.

But the big reason I use a home analogy is because you can invite someone in to *experience* it.

Creating your home (brand) should be seen as creating an experience for you and your guests (your employees and customers). You can think of it in terms of inviting someone into your domain, to interact with your business through those "thousand gestures".

As is the case with a well-ordered home where the front door has to work with the door frame, the hallway, the walls and the rest of the building, your logo needs to work with your website, your sales brochure and your business card. Not to mention everything else that eventually follows as you build your brand piece by piece.

BRANDING FOR SMALL BUSINESSES

I've seen many small businesses put off by the notion of branding.

At the startup phase of a business, usually with one or two people sharing an office, these owners feel branding doesn't apply to them – that it's only something for bigger companies and conglomerates to concern themselves with.

I'd argue that it is just as important for startups and small businesses to get their branding right in order to project themselves with clarity and consistency through the "noise" of all the so-called bigger, established corporations.

KEY POINTS

- A brand is an interface between an organisation and a group of people. It creates an experience or a set of experiences for those people.

- Branding can be split into brand essence and brand expression.

- Successful brands consistently deliver the same brand essence in different ways, across multiple touch points.

- Graphic design is used to create a large part of a brand's expression.

- A graphic designer has the power to take you from being an intangible idea into a tangible entity that interacts with customers.

CHAPTER 2
The value of branding

AUTHORITY

Picture this: You click with someone at a trade show and immediately feel they are knowledgeable, smart and worth getting to know better. *And* they have the product you've been looking for! They seem like the perfect person to do business with.

At what stage would you start to lose confidence in this person and their business? When you find out they don't have a business card? When you see that they don't have a brochure? When you look them up on the Internet and find out they don't even have a website?

What if it's *you* who doesn't have those basic elements in place? At the most fundamental level, branding gets you in the game and allows you to participate on a professional level. It enables you to look established right from the get go, giving your target audience a cushion of trust from which to start the relationship.

You have to see branding as a performance stage that you have built for yourself (with your graphic designer) from which to sing your message.

ATTRACTING INVESTORS AND PARTNERS

Branding your business, creates an asset that is unique to you in the market. If it is robust enough, that asset can be worth a lot of money.

A well-conceived and well-constructed brand offers instant scalability, because you have the principles and processes in place, systematized, locked down and ready to be replicated. This positions you well in the eyes of bigger brands in your industry that potentially want to buy you out. A brand, done properly, is highly attractive for investors and buyers.

Your brand will also enable you to attract the right people with whom to partner. When you elevate the status of your business through your branding, you project yourself as an organization worth doing business with. In turn it deters those who you probably wouldn't want to do business with – who aren't concerned about how they project themselves to the market.

Businesses without strong, well-considered branding rock up to the negotiating table stark naked.

"Hi! I'm looking for partners."

BETTER STAFF

Competent branding communicates not just with customers, partners, investors and the media, but also with your own current and future employees. It sets a standard for them and ensures that you are leading by example.

If you identify and craft a brand essence – a mission and a vision for your business – and communicate that through your workforce in an effective and compassionate way, you are creating the environment for a more coherent, caring and inspired workforce. Attracting and cultivating better staff inevitably leads to a higher level of customer service and a better experience for your customers.

Branding provides a structure and a series of reference points for staff, giving them a system they can rely on. This is vital when it comes to delivering that coveted consistency that leads to the compounding effect of a brand in people's minds.

SHOWING THAT YOU CARE

Considerate branding shows your target audience that you care about them, that you have spent time understanding their issues and that you know how to communicate to them on that level – you are fluent in *their* needs and *their* problems. This shows respect and is a crucial rapport-builder.

But a brand is a two-way interface, and gives you the opportunity not just to talk with your employees and target audience, but listen to them as well. The brands that get this right, who use their multiple touch points as listening devices as well as talking devices will always see great results. Richard Branson and Virgin are the masters of this type of interfacing.

SALES PLATFORM

Imagine yourself as a fruit and vegetable supplier. You have a whole bunch of produce to sell, so you take it down to the market. When you arrive you find there is no allocated spot, no table on which to set down your goods and no signage to point buyers to your business.

This is how unbranded businesses find themselves in the market. They have no table from which to sell their wares. A brand makes your business real and gives you a platform to interact with an audience and sell and deliver your business from.

Branding makes it easier for people to buy things from you on the literal level be that through e-commerce; signage to point people in the right direction (advertising); sales people who are versed in the brand's essence; sales forms and brochures; and all sorts of other systems that facilitate the sales process.

A brand is also an integral part of the product funnel for a business. When a website is well designed and communicates the correct information in a logical manner for the user, that user cannot help but feel they are already benefitting from the interaction. This means you are perceived as an abundant provider of your particular product or service – that your well of knowledge and expertise is deep and that your core offering is extraordinary.

REAL ESTATE

Have a quick scan through your mind and look for brands that spring to the front of your consciousness, for whatever reason.

It is fair to say that for the majority of people, things like Nike, Starbucks, Apple, Microsoft, BP, Shell, adidas, McDonalds, Mercedes, The Gap, Gucci and Coca-Cola will emerge. In true stereotypical fashion, some women might put more clothes brands to the fore, some men might put more emphasis on car and/or technology brands.

These are the superbrands, powerful interfaces that evoke something inside of us. These superbrands own real estate in our conscious and sub-conscious minds!

Superbrands are built up in our heads by subtle (and sometimes not so subtle) carefully thought-out, constant reminders. Consistent, multiple touch points have allowed them to own time and space in the minds of their audiences.

As small and medium sized businesses, we can play a similar game when we focus on extremely narrow target audiences, often referred to as micro niches. We too can own a certain amount of real estate in the minds of the people that matter most to our businesses.

Shaa Wasmund, founder of Smarta.com, uses a compelling illustration when talking about building our personal influence which I think can be applied to branding.

She says you can either be a dot in someone's mind or you can create a line. If you catch someone's attention with one piece of information, you are a dot in their stream of consciousness (see illustration right). But if you create a series of dots or touch points you start to create a line and become more noticeable until eventually, they know who you are and what you are about.

All the dots that are not linked represent different businesses trying to grab one person's attention with one-off pieces of promotional material. These are just dots, blips in the mind of the target.

The value of branding

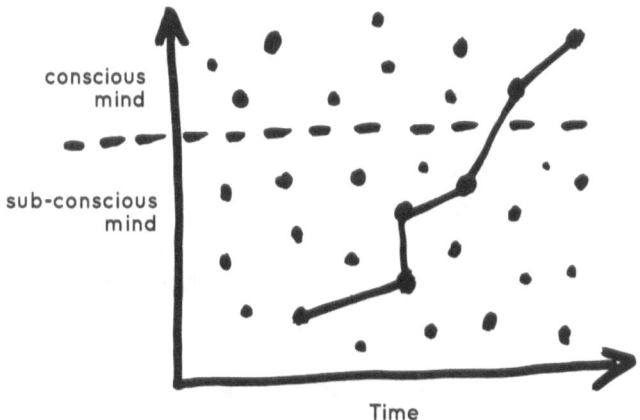

The linked dots represent the activities of one business creating multiple touch points that are relevant to each other (through the brand) and to the person. These join up to create a line that eventually sticks out in the conscious mind of the person. (Note: I have added the distinction between the conscious and sub-conscious mind to Wasmund's illustration.)

A brand provides you with the medium to keep people up-dated on what you're up to; keep them educated on why they need your product or service; and nurture their confidence in you as a provider.

Creating real estate in the minds of your target audience differentiates you from the competition. By spending time growing this real estate you mark out and own the specific territory that makes you unique.

What's also fantastic about this approach to marketing is that it is non-invasive. Done systematically over time, your touch points become a part of your prospects' lives and your brand sits comfortably with them not just up until the moment they buy, but beyond.

SAVING TIME

What if the world's greatest composers throughout history never wrote down their music but kept it in their heads until they died? There would be no legacy. It would also mean that every time some duke or monarch wanted their music to be played, they would have to physically show up and spend hours communicating their ideas to orchestras and choirs before giving a performance and sharing their music with the public.

Countless business owners without a well-devised brand submit themselves to a similarly torturous process. Branding translates the genius in your head into a replicable set of key messages onto a page, website, banner, brochure, app, etc. Once you are clear on your brand essence you can replicate your message across multiple platforms. It can then be translated across all the formats that your market either responds to most or is able to adopt most readily.

This saves you time on several levels:

- You don't have to keep on having the same conversations with prospects. You can simply direct them to the relevant content you have created as part of your interface. As long as your brand is strong enough, you can rely on it to have those repetitious conversations for you.

- It takes a lot of leg-work out of the sales conversion. You don't spend excessive amounts of time convincing people that you are the right person for the job.

- When your brand shows the world that you are serious about what you do, the time-wasters go elsewhere. A brand sorts the wheat from the chaff when it comes to prospects. You attract customers who are willing to pay for the level of quality you have communicated up front.

A well-conceived brand saves time for your target audience too. When you communicate your offer concisely and precisely and to the people who actually care, they can make decisions much faster on whether you are right for them or not.

STORY-TELLING

You need to capture your target audience's attention and imagination. The best way to do this is by telling a story through your branding.

At the time of writing, Chiki Tea is a startup based in the UK and specializes in all things to do with Japanese tea. Products include: a book; a tea steeping kit: the tea itself; tea-inspired stationary and greeting cards; tea salons; certification programmes; and trips to Japan.

In terms of positioning the business in the hearts and minds of consumers, we wanted it to be clear that Chiki Tea is less about Japanese tea the commodity and more about the wonders and mysticism of Japan itself.

For this reason we came up with the tag line "introducing the magical world of Japanese tea". This allows Chiki Tea to pivot from one product, tea for instance, all the way to stationary and organized trips to Japan, without breaking the link to the heart of what Chiki Tea does.

The concept for the branding is based on the story of how Yan Emperor Shennong discovered tea. Possibly a mythical figure living 5,000 years ago, Shennong was a herbalist who roamed Asia with his servants, experimenting with plants, fruits and herbs.

Legend has it that one day Shennong was meditating, when a leaf from the *Camellia sinensis* plant landed in his cup of boiling water and infused it. Shennong, in his spiritual wisdom, knew that all things were as they should be, and instead of removing the leaf and tossing out the sullied water, drank from his cup and tea was born.

This wonderful story underpins the branding for Chiki Tea. In chapter 5 you will be able to see how the branding works across various elements such as the Chiki Tea business card and website.

This is how value is created in the hearts and minds of customers through a story. Far from being yet another company that sells tea, Chiki Tea positions itself as something more magical, more intriguing, more informative than a company selling a commoditea!

But brand stories can be more subtly disguised.

Storm DJs rents equipment and DJs to private parties and events. The shape of the icon in the logo (top right) is derived from a "story", a piece of rationale about how the brand expression should work.

The name of the business suggested that we create something to do with storms and/or DJs (!). But there needed to be a twist, something to tap into the essence of what Storm DJs are really about. They aren't about DJs and DJ equipment, they are about creating the energy that makes a great party.

STORM DJS

MUSIC OF A HIGHER ORDER

The shape of the logo is an abstraction of a storm cloud with a lightening bolt coming out of it. But it also echoes the shape of the notation chemists use to describe the neurotransmitter serotonin (below), believed to be associated with happiness and well-being.

As subliminal as it might be, the story behind Storm DJs' brand expression pitches the business as a high value product rather than a low value commodity. The true value of Storm DJs lives in what they *provide* to party hosts: party guests having a good time! It does not necessarily live in what they "provide": DJs and DJ equipment.

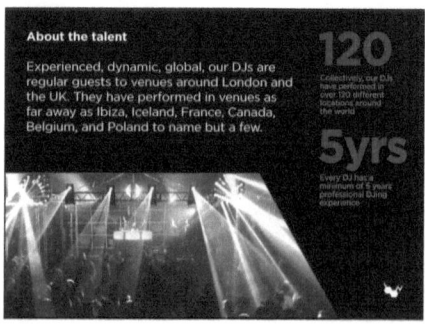

The value of branding

This concept is then transposed throughout the rest of the marketing to create a consistent experience for the target audience. Notice how the graphic device is either used to frame the imagery or is echoed in the lighting and other objects in the photographs themselves.

The concept always has to come from the brand essence to be strong. Getting this right is one of the trickiest aspects of good branding, but it is also the most rewarding.

If you would like to see full case studies (in colour) of the Chiki Tea and Storm DJs branding as well as some more projects, please visit our website: **www.ashfordperkins.com**

BRANDING AND MONEY

The word brand originally came from the Old Norse "brandr", meaning to burn. Back then, it meant to literally burn a mark onto livestock to aid traders in distinguishing between cattle. Interestingly, it seems that it was around this time that the reputation of a "business entity" became associated with a brandr.

For instance, a farmer who was known for the high quality of animals he brought to market would find his "branded" cattle sought after. In contrast, those whose livestock had less of a good reputation would find their cattle (and their brandr) shunned and consequently sold for less.

With the birth of "brand", came a method of identifying and perceiving value.

Created in our minds, brands are personal experiences because what we value in life is personal.

It was the economist Alfred Marshall (1842 – 1924) who once talked about how we can put a monetary value on any conceivable thing. Originally referring to human capital, Marshall inferred that, hypothetically, you could pay somebody to do just about anything provided the price was right.

So for instance, you could pay a non-smoker $100 to smoke a cigarette. With someone else, you might have to pay $1,000, but they would still have a threshold at which they would eventually value owning $1,000 over the discomfort of, or the infringement of their principles involved with smoking that cigarette. Yet another person might yield at $10,000. And this, the theory goes, could be applied to anything and everyone ad infinitum.

However tenuous this might seem to you as a theory

for human behaviour, it highlights an interesting, although certainly not ground breaking, idea:

When your customer buys something from you, they are valuing your product more than the money they are willing to part with.

The question is, which product are you currently pitching to your target market?

Using Storm DJs as an example, are you pitching the equivalent of "DJs and DJ equipment" (low value) or are you pitching "happy party guests" (high value)?

Using Chiki Tea as an example, are you pitching "Japanese tea" (low value) or are you pitching the "magical world of Japanese tea" (high value)?

If you are a business coach, are you pitching coaching (commodity) or the ability to bust through fear (high value product)?

If you are a personal trainer, are you pitching workouts (commodity) or are you pitching life transformation (high value product).

Take a look at your own products. It is possible that your pricing strategy reflects the value you currently

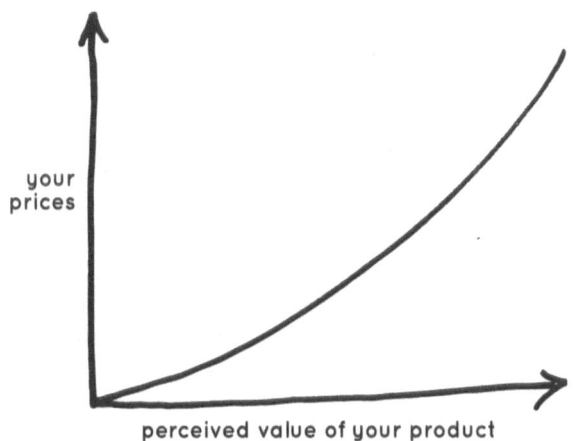

project towards your target audience.

This shift alone, from viewing your offering as a commodity to a high value product, can transform a business almost instantly (provided the branding is right to communicate it).

Ask yourself: is your current branding communicating the value you really want to project or is it pitching a product (reflected in your pricing) with a lower value attached to it?

Finding your "true value" is directly correlated with identifying your essence.

The value of branding

KEY POINTS

- Branding gives you visibility in the market and projects your business as trustworthy, consistent and professional.

- A brand gives you a replicable, scalable set of systems, making you more attractive to investors and partners and making it easier for staff to get aligned with your mission.

- Your branding can show your audience that you respect and care about them.

- Good branding will attract the calibre of investors, partners, staff, and customers you want.

- Story-telling delights, informs and educates your target market. It is also the vehicle through which you communicate your essence.

- When you are properly branded, you pitch a high quality product or service to market rather than a commodity, hence elevating yourself out of the dog-fight of price wars.

CHAPTER 3
What to brand, when to brand

Branding has to fulfil a specific purpose that serves your business. Each touch point that you create needs to have a reason to exist. Producing marketing collateral that isn't needed or that is mal-conceived is wasteful and potentially harmful.

BRANDING NEEDS TO SERVE YOUR BUSINESS, NOT THE OTHER WAY AROUND

I'll never forget the time I was working at a studio in London, which had just won some new work. The brief was to brand a business with a new concept for on-line dating. The client threw all of his personal savings at the project, certain that he was backing a winner.

The studio readily accepted the project and proceeded in designing a logo, a website and a whole host of other marketing materials. Every now and then the client would come in and have a meeting to see how we were getting along. Then one day, out of the blue, the project got cancelled. The client had run out of cash. He had confused creating a brand with having a business model. Rather than the branding serving his business objective, the capital for his business had funded a stand-alone graphic design project.

To avoid scenarios that resemble anything near this

travesty, you need to get clear on how the branding is going to improve your business, not destroy it.

The first conversations I have with my own clients are all about the business itself: how it operates; what it does; what the best-selling products are; how effective the sales process is; where the weaknesses lie; what the strengths are; etc.

I turn businesses away when I realize that it's not a branding expert they need, it's a financial advisor, or a business coach. Hopefully the previous chapter will have given you an idea of the key areas in which branding works to improve business. But that doesn't mean the timing for implementing a brand infrastructure is the same for everyone.

You need to evaluate whether or not the time is right for you. You also need to determine whether it's simply more graphic design you need (i.e. some brochures or flyers) under your current branding or whether it's a fully-fledged branding or re-branding process.

START FROM YOUR DESTINATION

You'd never take a flight without having a destination in mind and the same goes for branding your business. You need to know where you're going in order to get there!

If you are not sure about your business's "destination", map out your vision on a large sheet of paper. Start out in big picture-mode, whether that's a multi-billion dollar empire or the six-figure small business from home. Write it down and draw it out starting from the **right** hand side.

Now working back in increments that are most realistic, write down landmarks in the development and growth of your business that enable you to get to the next step. Do this until you come all the way back down to where you are today, which will be on the left hand side of the page. Label each increment as a stage, starting with today as stage 1 and ascending to however many stages you have on the page.

On the right is an example of how a client and I planned his next course of action, by starting at the right side of the page with his grand vision for the business. I have labeled the stages one to five with a marker pen for the sake of this illustration.

What to brand, when to brand

As you look over the completed plan, consider each stage a short- to medium-term goal that you need to focus on before reaching the next one as you move towards the right of the page. You should be able to evaluate what it is that you must accomplish in order to reach your next landmark. This could be anything depending on what your business is and where you are in the journey.

The next thing you need could be:

- a well-designed presentation with mock-ups of products to show investors for raising capital;

- a Facebook page to build a community;

- an e-commerce website;

- a sales brochure;

- a fully-fledged branding process.

It could be a combination of all of the above as well as a whole host of other things that need designing.

But, it could be none of the above – it could be nothing to do with branding. It might be you need to go out to China to source new items for your product range.

It might be that you need to hire someone who can help you with your admin or distribution. It might be you need a mentor or a cleaner or a chauffeur or a masseuse!

This might seem like a banal exercise for some of you, but if done properly, it saves you time and money because you don't focus on the wrong thing for your business at this stage of its development.

Sketching out your company's growth and highlighting the landmarks means that you can see what you may need further down the line. It gives you an idea about what to prioritise in a very clear and visual way.

A QUICK CHECK LIST TO HELP YOU

Here are a few questions you may want to ask yourself to determine whether you need branding or re-branding and to what degree. They are all relevant:

- Where are you right now and where do you want to get to? What is your destination?

- What is your most profitable product? Do you need to put more attention into marketing this or do you see an opportunity in creating a new offering? What else could you be doing for your customers right now?

- Who are your best customers and why do they like buying from you? How and when do they buy from you? Do you have a healthy amount of repeat custom?

- Have your customers explicitly commented on your current branding (or lack thereof)? Conducting an on-line survey is an easy way of finding out what they think.

- Is your business directed towards other businesses (B2B) or towards consumers (B2C)? Depending on your sector, it could be that you don't need the same degree of branding if you are B2B that you will most certainly need if you are B2C. For instance, as a B2B business, the logo in particular may not be as important to focus on getting right at this moment in time. A well-structured PowerPoint presentation or sales brochure might be your priority.

As a B2C business though, your logo will be more important, especially if your products are on store shelves. That is when your logo needs to be a stand out, big, throbbing button to attract your audience's attention and will be central to the success of your brand.

- As a follow on from the previous point, ask yourself: how does my target audience best like to engage with us? Focus on developing and perfecting the specific touch points that yield the most results.

- If you are at the start up phase, do you need to slow down before getting all those brochures printed and evaluate whether you have identified and articulated a brand essence? Would this help you with your positioning? Or are you happy to proceed with your marketing anyway?

- What are the strengths, weaknesses, opportunities and threats to your organization? What do you see on the horizon? What is the next big thing in your industry? How will you need to respond? Where will the industry be in the next ten years? What are your competitors up to? Do a SWOT analysis to gain insight into your business and the surrounding landscape.

The big questions that I always ask clients before proceeding with a project of any size are:

- What is the purpose of what you want to create?

- What do you want to get out of it?

KEY POINTS

- Your brand needs to serve your business, not the other way around.

- If a touch point doesn't play a specific role in the growth of your business, question whether it needs to be there and be prepared to ditch it. Each touch point that you create needs to be there for a reason.

- Two important questions to ask yourself before proceeding with a project: What is the purpose of what you want to create? What benefits do you want to get from it?

CHAPTER 4
The all-important brand essence

USING A GRAPHIC DESIGNER

A significant amount of your branding will need to be created by a graphic designer, so it is important to spend the effort finding a talented one.

When choosing a graphic designer, you should be aware of how sensitive he/she is to your business' needs. Make sure you communicate to them the true value – the brand essence – of your business before you write a brief for them. Sometimes they might be savvy enough to develop your brand essence with you: that's when you know you've struck gold with your graphic designer! But just like mining for gold, it's rare to find. Your brand strategist's role is to do this.

Unfortunately, graphic designers can sometimes lose track of what you are trying to achieve as a business by getting caught up in the *art* of it all.

In the real world, there have been examples of beautifully creative design work released into the public that have failed to deliver on the business challenge that the branding was meant to solve.

I was recently asked to comment on a piece of branding for a business owner because something was niggling at her. The minimalistic, carefully crafted, and highly conceptual work was visually stunning. It set the client apart from the competition because it was so stylish, unique and polished.

But I asked her the following: **"does this branding build rapport with your target audience? Does it convey to them your ability to empathize with their issues? And does it clearly show how your product adds value to their lives?"** When I asked her these questions, she immediately understood why it had been bugging her.

This business owner knew something was not quite right, but she wasn't able to put her finger on it. She also knew it looked fantastic, was done by one of the world's top branding agencies, and therefore was confused about the mixed feelings she had for the designs.

In this instance, the branding had been created to win a graphic design award within the creative industry. It had not been created to sell the client's high value product to her customers. This is a classic case of a graphic designer or design agency producing work as an exercise in self-glorification rather than addressing the client's real-life business needs.

There can be a difference between design work that

looks amazing purely on its own merit and effective branding that sells your high-value product. Knowing the difference is key but also challenging. Feel free to ask your designer and yourself the same questions I put to the business owner in the anecdote above.

I've observed other pitfalls when clients and graphic designers fail to work well with each other:

- clients feeling as if the graphic designer has not listened to them;

- designers producing marketing collateral that the client doesn't need but ends up paying for because they don't know how to contest it;

- designers getting offended when the client confronts them on the aesthetic or even functional aspects of the branding.

But the worst thing is when any of the above gets in the way of having your business branded properly.

HOW TO USE A GRAPHIC DESIGNER PROPERLY

The more you understand the creative process, the better the relationship you will have with your designer.

When you brief a graphic designer, you put information into their head. They then draw upon all the knowledge and personal experience they have gleaned from the past and combine that with your brief and the skills they have at their disposal to create something for you.

Generally, but not always, small and medium sized businesses will approach a graphic designer and say: "I am an osteopath, I need a business card" or "I am an accountant, please design a website for me".

This is not the rich and engaging information needed to ignite true creativity. A graphic designer should be a creative individual in the first place but they still need to be inspired. Your job is to ignite their flame, to breathe life into the creative process in order to get the results you dream of.

The best racing cars in the world still need petrol to function in the same way a graphic designer needs adequate fuel to be able to fire on all cylinders for you.

The all-important brand essence

The typical small business approach.

The all-important brand essence

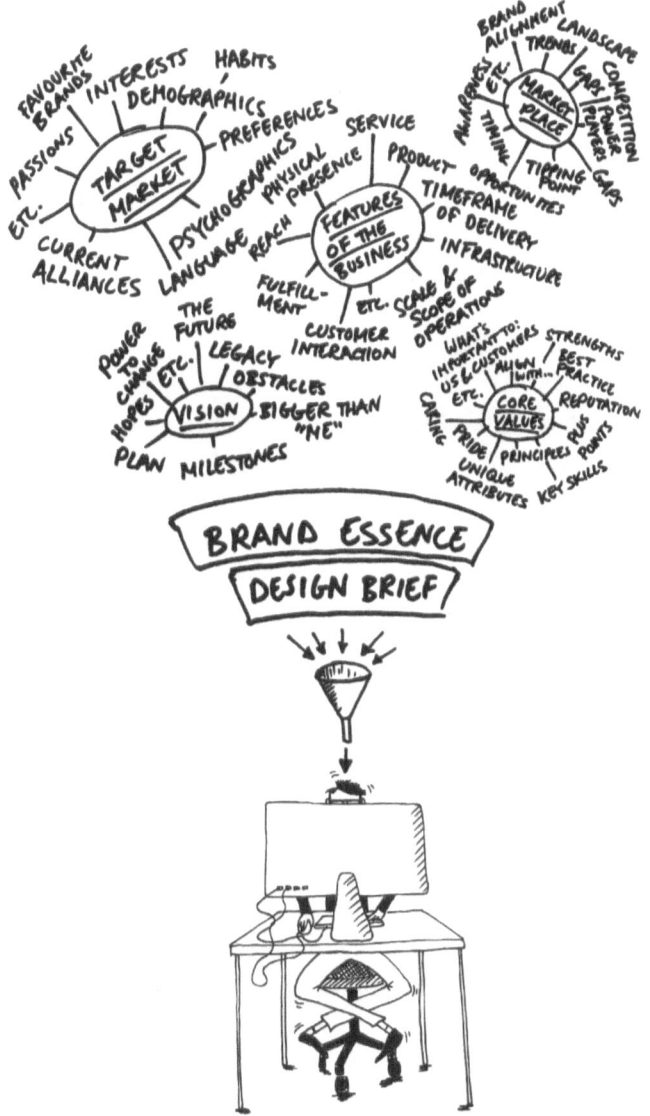

The typical superbrand approach.

The all-important brand essence

Unfortunately, there will always be a designer out there who is willing to oblige a small business owner brandishing a miserly brief without any further questioning. The result is often a poor piece of design, not even worth calling branding, that does little to communicate their true value and help grow their business.

Large brands and certainly superbrands use graphic designers very differently. Not only do they use teams of designers, often with highly focused specialities within the team, but they understand that because graphic design is used to build huge portions of the interface, a fair bit of planning needs to go into it. The creative director and graphic designers need to be aligned to the business' needs; the strategy; and a whole raft of other material that will give them the context within which to work and from which to draw inspiration.

When the brand essence is brought to life, target markets and competitors are identified; core values and mission statements are written; attributes and features are listed; and visions and stories are outlined.

And then they brief* the designer which inevitably leads to more robust branding.

The richer and more accurate the information you feed into the graphic designer's brain, the more you are stacking the odds in your favour.

*We cover the graphic design brief in more detail in Chapter 5.

THE BLACK BOX

The creative process involved in a branding project is quite extraordinary when you think about it. The graphic designer takes your brand essence and translates it into your brand expression.

Analogous to a black box situation, information about your company goes in one end and something real and tangible comes out the other.

As a graphic designer myself, I have been blessed to have experienced (and been conscious of) this magical process many a time. But like all graphic designers, I've had just as many experiences where it goes badly wrong and creative blocks set in to halt the progress.

One of my most vivid memories of the creative process going well harks back to a time when I was still freelancing at studios around London. I was called into an agency to create the graphics for a big stage screen for a gala dinner held in honour of the Football Writers' Association sponsored by Barclays.

There was no brief for me to read or digest, rather I was simply told that I needed to create something they could use for the event. But, thanks to my love of football and my knowledge of the subject as well as the Barclays brand, I found it unusually easy to deliver a compelling concept and execute on it quickly.

This is more or less what happened: I knew I had to create a series of graphic images linking the act of writing with the game of football. In my mind I saw an old-fashioned ink well, the sort you would use with a quill pen. And suddenly all this ink came flying out of the well, high up into the air and then tumbling down onto the paper beneath.

As this was happening I heard all these journalists shouting their stories out loud, yelling over each other. Through the cacophony of sound, I picked out fragments of sentences and as the ink splashed down on the page it created images of footballers playing the beautiful game along with pull outs of the quotes from the writers.

The ink (Barclays' deep blue of course!) from the writers' pens was recreating the most memorable moments from the season. I sat down with my own

The all-important brand essence

pen, a scanner, a disk of images and a mac and the project just flowed out of me.

In this instance, I didn't need a strategic brief. I was clear on the essence of what needed to be communicated and I was able to draw on my own knowledge of the sport to fill in the gaps and get inspired.

But this was not a fully-fledged branding job and I had managed to get away with it that time. A few days later, at the same studio, I was asked to design, you guessed it, a full rebrand for a private equity firm. At the time I didn't even know what private equity was. True to the ethos of the studio where I was working, this project had no robust brief or preliminary strategy.

It was agony as I wrestled with trying to deliver a powerful concept for a business in a field I knew nothing about and had no brief to refer to. I failed miserably in delivering something that could pass as a respectable piece of designed communication.

BRANDING DONE RIGHT VERSUS BRANDING DONE WRONG

There's no way a lot of startups and small businesses can afford paying for the amount of strategy that goes into the superbrands. But the good news is there are compromises that can be made and best practices that can be drawn from.

The following short story has been devised to show you how, by taking the right approach, you can have a decent brand pop out on the other side of some thorough discussion and exploration around your business.

Meet Jim.

For the past ten years, Jim has coached women in Rhythmic Gymnastics*. During this time, Jim has become intrigued by how toned and muscular his students get, especially from the work they do with the ribbon.

---

* Rhythmic Gymnastics is a sport that combines elements of ballet, gymnastics, dance and apparatus manipulation. It involves the use of five pieces of apparatus – ball, ribbon, hoop, clubs, rope – on a floor mat, with a much greater emphasis on the aesthetic rather than the acrobatic.

Ribbon looks like this:

Jim has discovered that when *men* partake in ribbon workouts, the results are twice as impressive.

This has given Jim a business idea!

He wants to create the first-ever ribbon fitness programme for men only. The idea is audacious to say the least! How will men respond to this new product?

Jim has the uncomfortable feeling that he's going to need some flyers to market his workouts.

So he knocks some up on Word, prints them out and hands them to people on the street.

No one bites.

A friend suggests he gets a logo designed, so Jim sees if the internet can provide him with a quick and easy solution. He is keen to get this out of the way so that he can get back to the more important aspects of running his business.

He discovers a website called Robot-Operated Baloney-Based Emergency Design (ROBBED). All Jim has to do is type in the name of his company "Jim's Gym" with a brief explanation of what his business does.

On the other side of the planet a robot devises a positioning statement for Jim: "Ribbon for men. It makes you fitter and stronger"; selects a font for his business name; evaluates what colours should be used; puts the finishing touches to the crafted icon and sends it back, all within three seconds, costing Jim $150. It's a total bargain.

The logo looks like this:

The all-important brand essence

"Phew!" says Jim. "Thank goodness that's over with."

Jim puts the logo on his flyers and hits the street once again.

This time he gets a response: a skinhead tries to beat him up! Luckily, Jim can handle himself so all is not lost. Apart from the kerfuffle, nothing else emerges, certainly not the leads Jim is looking for.

His business starts to suffer.

ENTER SALVATION

Meet Sal.

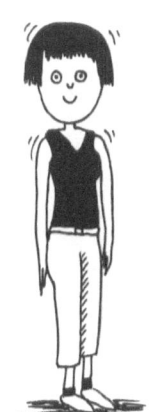

Sal is a brand strategist who works with a select few graphic designers to create brands for small and medium sized businesses. A mutual friend introduces Jim to her.

Jim explains the problem to Sal and she immediately gets it:

"Look Jim. I get it," she says. "It seems to me that you are lacking the following:

- the articulation of a brand essence determined by who your target audience is and how you serve them at the deepest of levels;

- a story or set of stories that illuminate your brand essence through your brand expression;
- an outline of the deliverables that are needed to communicate to your target audience;

- a properly structured brief for the graphic designer...

... in fact, wait a minute, did you go to RUBBED for this?"

The next morning, Sal and Jim reconvene.

BRAND ESSENCE – THE SEEDS OF A STORY

Sal starts by unearthing the true value that Jim brings to market – the essence of Jim's brand. She asks him to talk her through what it is that his customers get from his product.

As the conversation develops, she begins to see what drives not only Jim's business but Jim himself.

Sal discovers that ribbon combines the constant shifting of bodily weight with a fantastic cardio-vascular workout. According to Jim, Ribbon enhances blood flow throughout the entire circulatory system, more so than any other type of fitness training.

This enhanced blood flow invigorates people, giving them renewed confidence and mental clarity as well as a well-toned body. It seems that men in particular benefit when they take this renewed energy and confidence back into their workplace and into their family lives. Their lives change for the better.

Sal realises that this is all about a new lifestyle. She

identifies Jim's *real* product as feelings of elevated confidence and mental clarity (high value) and not what he has been focussing on in his marketing: ribbon workouts (low value).

She grills Jim on who his target audience is. He thinks its men, but Sal says that this is too vague. Jim doesn't have the marketing budget to blast his message through the main advertising platforms such as television and billboards, so he needs to focus on a smaller group and be clever about how he's going to approach them.

They identify a primary target market that Jim's branding will need to address: men who lack confidence at work and in other social situations, typically aged between 23 and 35 years old.

By this stage Jim is also starting to see his business in a new light.

"What do you think of the name?" he asks Sal.

"Jim's Gym?" she replies. "It's awful! Look, you understand your own business much better now, just by having this conversation. I'm sure we can come up with something that reflects the true value you bring to your customers in a more meaningful way."

The all-important brand essence

After much discussion and debate, they settle for **Ripped Ribbon** (!) with the positioning statement "New-found power from within".

"This is your brand essence, Jim." Sal exclaims. "You are in the business of helping your customers tap into their ultimate self. You are about empowering young men and helping them forge new paths in their life."

Jim feels a surge of excitement rush through his body. He realises that he has just repositioned his business from quirky (or downright weird) workouts to scientifically backed, results-driven fitness training.

Jim is clear on his target audience, why his business is valuable to them, and how to position it in the hearts and minds of his customers.

This is a tremendous relief for him. He jumps up and does several pirouettes to celebrate.

"Let's go for a beer!" he shouts. "Um! I mean a carrot juice. Of course …"

"Wait up!" Sal interrupts. "There's just a few more things we need to straighten out and then we can be on our way.

THE DELIVERABLES AND THE GRAPHIC DESIGN BRIEF

"Jim, it's obvious now that you are going to be needing more than a few flyers to promote your business, don't you think?"

Jim knows Sal is right. All this brand essence stuff is fine in the confines of a strategic conversation with an expert, but how will that translate into growing his business?

Sal acknowledges Jim's panicked look.

"Jim, all we need to do is work out how your audience is going to find you. For a start, you will have to project yourself as a credible business. You will need a logo, and a business card. Otherwise people just won't take you seriously.

"These days too, you absolutely have to have a website. People will be checking you out on Google. What else do you think we need? How else do you think we can reach your audience consisting of shy, unconfident men?"

"What about a DVD?" says Jim. " These guys need to experience my workouts from the comfort of their own home before venturing out and committing themselves to something so drastic!"

"Great thinking Jim" says Sal. "Let's do it!"

After fleshing out a brief for Sal's graphic designers, they schedule a meeting for a few weeks time so that the designers can put together some options for Jim.

Two weeks later, Sal shows Jim a range of logos along with some mood boards and additional visuals of how Jim's brand story will carry across the various touch points of his brand through a concept.

After some deliberation, Jim opts for this one:

"I love the way it shows the strength, presence and confidence of the participant," exclaims Jim. "And the concept tells the story of enhanced blood flow throughout the body's circulatory system perfectly while hinting at the ribbon itself."

"That's great!" Sal beams. "Notice the font I have selected for your business name and the positioning statement. It's a solid, strong typeface that oozes confidence and compliments the icon.

The all-important brand essence

"Now that you have chosen your preferred concept we will proceed with implementing it across your business card, website and DVD boxset."

A few more weeks go by and when Jim visits Sal next, he finds himself in branding heaven!

"Look at how the logo and the graphic device of the ribbon work across all of your collateral." says Sal.

"This your business card (front and back) :

The all-important brand essence

"and this is your website:

"and your DVD boxset.

"See how your brand essence is reflected in each touch point and how the concept ties everything together to tell a consistent brand story? This is how branding works as a whole. It gives the customer a sense of being in your business and being part of it.

"There is a seamless transition when someone puts down your business card to visit the website. These touch-points will combine and contribute to your target audience's perception of what your business does and *why* it is valuable to them – everything pivots

The all-important brand essence

from your brand essence."

We leave the story of Jim and Sal here. Suffice to say, Jim's brand grows in lock step with his business. As Jim employs more people, he has Sal's designers create employee manuals and uniforms.

He and Sal audit the customer experience and devise new ways of improving each and every touch-point. As Jim goes out to present his business to investors and partners, he gets Sal's agency to design presentation slides and printed leave-behinds.

Each touch point or gesture Jim creates stems from the heart of his business and reflects the true value he brings to market. Every action, product, marketing piece ties back to his essence and if it doesn't, it is quickly scrapped.

Jim starts to appreciate that branding is synonymous with business development.

Jim now loves branding!

The end.

This is an oversimplified outline of a strategic and creative process. It is also a very loose and carefree approach and one that some business owners can find disconcerting. It is an approach that I use with a lot of my own clients but it doesn't work for everyone. For this reason I acknowledge that for some of my clients, I need to take a more scientific approach to avoid losing them altogether.

There are thousands, if not tens of thousands of different methodologies out there and I hope that by introducing you to one of my preferred alternative methods I am covering a fairly broad spectrum of preferences.

A MORE SCIENTIFIC APPROACH

Having researched and sat through all sorts of methodologies, I have identified an approach that I think works very well. It delivers a brand essence in a more structured and, some would argue, less haphazard way of working!

I have access to this process thanks to its creators Peter Thomson and Klaus Bravenboer. Thomson is a business strategist who advises technology companies on social media and Bravenboer is a brand strategist working with entrepreneurs. Bravenboer is the founder of a brand strategy agency called Fuel Story:

www.fuelstory.com

Thomson and Bravenboer call this new approach to creating a brand essence the bow-tie model. The bow-tie model takes a traditional brand pyramid and mirrors it with an external communications framework. In my mind, this fleshes out the staid pyramid model with a dose of practical messaging that can be implemented

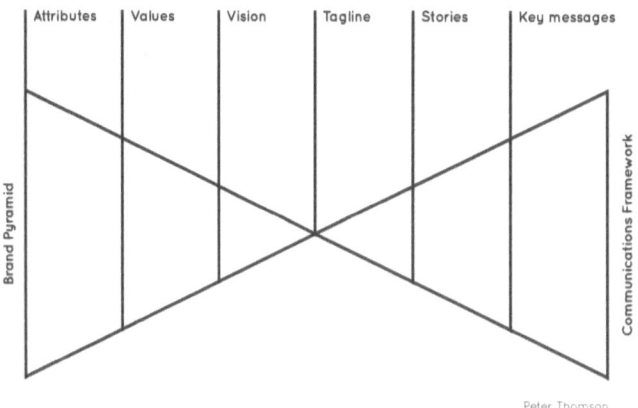

faster than traditional brand essence techniques.

This process takes more than a few hours of conversation to get the most out of it. Depending on the size of the project, it usually takes a full day of exploration and a fair amount work needs to be done prior to and post the work done with the business owner.

You start at the left hand side and work through identifying the attributes, the values and the vision of the business. You then hop over to the far right and work on articulating the key messages and the stories that ignite the brand culminating in a positioning statement (or tagline to use Fuel Story's language).

The system is methodical and rigorous and provides business owners with a structure to support their thinking and from which to derive their rationale. For more on the bow tie model, see Thomson's blog post here: **http://tinyurl.com/96yvoy5**

KEY POINTS

- Feed your graphic designer's head with quality content. The richer the information, the richer the expression.

- Understand who your target audience is and how you serve them. They often hold the key to your brand essence.

- Look for a story or set of stories that illuminate your brand essence through your brand expression.

- For a more methodical approach to defining your brand essence use the Fuel Story bow tie model and work through the attributes, values, vision, key messages, stories, and tagline.

Note: If you are reading this in the hope of finding your brand essence and feel as if you are still not clear, there is a series of exercises at the end of the book that could give you more insight.

CHAPTER 5
Eight steps to getting branded

Like it or not, there are some fundamental branding needs that, as a serious business owner, you just can't ignore. It doesn't matter how many followers you have on Twitter or how many people like you on Facebook (or not). It doesn't matter how au fait you are with the latest technology or digital platform (or not). At the very least, you must have:

• A logo;

• website;

• business cards.

Some people would say that a sales brochure needs to be there too, but for the purpose of this chapter, we'll look at these three items.

Also, I would say that in less than five years from now most businesses of any size will have to throw an app (software applications for mobile devises) into this essential mix in order to look like a serious business.

This is good news for small and medium sized businesses who might feel intimated by the idea of having to "build a brand" in order to exist in the market place. At this stage of your development you just have to cover these three elementary bases to make an impression, coordinate your marketing and, consequently grow from there.

Having these three elements created for you by a graphic designer is just the beginning of your brand building. These components will determine the look and feel of the rest of your marketing collateral further down the line.

There will be no need to keep reinventing the wheel. Nor should you because that would erode the all-important consistency we are looking for in your brand expression. Getting it right at this stage will set you up perfectly for the future.

Just as there are different ways to slice a cake, there are different ways to approach a branding project. I have distilled ten years of my experience working at big branding agencies and with small businesses, into a concise and fuss-free 8-step process to help you look like a pro!

The eight steps are:

Eight steps to getting branded

STEP 1
Strategic conversation(s) between you (the client) and the graphic designer

STEP 2
Write a brief for the graphic designer (your task)

STEP 3
The designer presents rough concepts (visuals) to you

STEP 4
Make a decision as to which concept you want implemented

STEP 5
The designer presents full designs of the logo, website and business card, using dummy copy (Lorem Ipsum)

STEP 6
You submit final content for the
website and business card

STEP 7
You sign off the designs and the designer
puts the project into artwork and production

STEP 8
Handover meeting between you
and the graphic designer

BONUS STEP
Follow up call with the graphic designer

Unless your designer has a readily defined project structure, I would suggest showing them this 8-Step template and asking them to adhere to it so that you are both clear on what to expect.

Let us explore each step in a little more detail.

STEP 1
Strategic conversation(s) between you (the client) and the graphic designer

There is no point in elaborating here. The most important subjects that need to be covered at this stage are in chapter 3 and 4. The strategic conversation(s) has to cover:

- **Why the project is needed**

- **Brand essence**

Needless to say, in conjunction with the content of this book, there is little point in progressing to step 2 before covering these bases.

You will also want to address the following:

Timings
Make sure you are clear about what your designer can achieve and by when. The more realistic both parties are about what they can achieve within a given time frame, the less nasty surprises tend to crop up.

What else is needed to initiate the project?
This is probably the most open-ended part of the brief

and is highly dependent on the project. Assuming you have addressed why the project is needed and have articulated the brand essence, here you can cover what further might be required to make the best out of the branding. For instance, you may feel the designer would benefit from experiencing your product or service first hand, or that a visit to your premises would give him/her that extra bit of insight.

Budget
How much money the project is going to cost and what the payment structure looks like. It is common that a graphic designer charges a deposit of say 30-50 per cent of the whole amount up front and invoices for the rest of the agreed amount just before the release of the project.

A note on budgeting for extra costs
It is important to note that a graphic designer might come up with a concept for a project that requires additional budget to implement. For instance, when presenting concepts to you in Step 3, one or some of those concepts might require commissioned or stock library photography or perhaps some illustrations, etc.

Or maybe incorporating an animation into your website will really bring a concept to life. These should be considered as additional charges that would need to be paid for separately and only with your consent. Make sure that at least one or two of the concepts presented in Step 3 require no additional cash to produce, although stock imagery of some sort is inevitably required for the website and further marketing materials.

STEP 2
Write a brief for the graphic designer (your task)

You wouldn't build a home without an architectural plan.

Think of a graphic design brief as the blueprint for your branding project. Without it, your branding is likely to turn out differently from how you wanted it.

Your brief should give the graphic designer a **context** within which your business operates and an indication of your destination (derived from the strategic conversation in Step 1). It must prescribe the branding you need with accuracy and clarity.

The following bullet points provide a broad template for a good brief for your graphic designer:

An overview of what the business does
This can be the executive summary taken from a business plan. It's the "what" of the business. Storm DJs supply DJs and sound equipment for private parties and events. Chiki Tea sells Japanese tea, courses on tea and trips to Japan. There is no mention yet of what I have been referring to as the "true value" or brand essence. The purpose here is clarity above all else. Get the graphic designer into the right ball park.

A description of the target audience
Be as specific as you can. The brand essence exercises at the end of the book give you a few ways to help determine who your target audience is.

The brand essence
Remember the purpose of explaining your brand essence to your graphic designer: **you want them to create concepts that tell your brand story in a compelling way**. Don't hold anything back here.

An overview of what is needed
These are the cold, hard deliverables. For the purpose of this chapter, you need to have the three elements we've been talking about, working in tandem to create a consistent experience: a logo; website; and a business card.

This stage can be broken down into several distinct parts of the project:

- In Step 3, the deliverables usually consist of three or four concepts for your branding.

  It would be too much work for the designer to give you finished versions of the logo, website and business card for all three or four concepts. What you need to see here is how the concept translates across the different components of your brand.

  This can be done in sketch form where the designer shows you several mood boards with shapes, colours, photographs, textures and styles he/she suggests could be used or maybe some computerized mock-ups of the business card and the home page of your website. At this stage you just want an idea of how the elements will work together.

- In Step 5, you choose a concept for the designer to implement. The deliverables will be finished designs for each component before they go into artwork and production.

- In Step 8, the deliverables will consist of the electronic files of the logo and business card as well as printed business cards and the uploaded website.

Acknowledgment of the competition
It is good practice to answer the following questions: Who is your competition? Where is your target audience already spending money? What are the similarities and what are the differences between you and your competition, in the way you operate and in the way you look and feel? What do you like and dislike about your competition's operations and their branding?

Strategic alignments
What brands are similar to yours in terms of aspirations and direction? Who are you planning to

partner with? What businesses will you need to sit next to and look on a par with?

Once the brief is submitted, the project has been initiated! The next thing you will see is your brand at its embryonic stage – the initial concepts. For many business owners this is a very exciting time. It's exhilarating to see ideas being born into reality, so enjoy this process! But remember, these are rough concepts that will likely require modification, sometimes combining two or more concepts into one.

STEP 3
The designer presents rough concepts (visuals) to you

Concepts are typically shown as rough versions of what the final branding could look like. A good way of understanding this stage is to think of it as the moment the graphic designer marks out the visual territory that you could own in the market place. Think back to the idea of building real estate in the minds of your audience – what should those "buildings" look and feel like?

With this in mind, resist looking at the details of the content (the specific imagery used, the typeface, even the colours) and focus more on whether the designer understood the *context* of what you are trying to achieve. Don't get put off of a good concept at this stage because you don't like the colours or a certain photo being used.

Ask yourself: Is there a concept that reflects the true value of my business?

On the following two pages you will see some of the initial concepts we showed one of our clients at this stage of her branding project. Broadway Barn is a 5-star bed and breakfast based in Ripley, Surrey. The thinking at this stage was all around pulling out the architectural features of Broadway Barn. As you will see in Step 4, further developments had to be made.

STEP 4

Make a decision as to which concept you want implemented

At this stage of the project, you have to decide (not on the spot) which concept you wish the designer to go ahead with and implement across your branding.

Eight steps to getting branded

The images used in the website mock-ups are courtesy of John-Paul Bland: www.jpbland.co.uk

The three photographs of the structural features of the barn (marked 1-3) were taken during the renovation of the buildings and in no way reflect the quality of the finished work.

All the other photographs were taken by myself and contributed to the mood boards and the creative process in some way.

Eight steps to getting branded

3

Having these concepts laid out in front of you should feel like surveying the land beneath you to find the best target on which to land. Think of landing right in the bull's eye of your target market!

In my mind, it's always best to meet your designer face to face so they can present their rough concepts to you either printed or on a screen.

Having said that, if your designer submits a PDF presentation with, say, four different concepts and one of them sings off the screen without any of your designer's verbal embellishment, perhaps you have the winner – perhaps you have an easy decision to make.

The complication arises when you're not quite sure of any of the designs, or maybe you like various aspects of one or some of them. This is when you must discuss with the designer what needs to be changed, thrown out, explored further, etc. This is why it is best that you are in the same room together, so that you can communicate as clearly as possible what you do and don't like.

It is important not to feel bullied or pressured into making a decision at this step. If you don't like any of the designs, say now or forever hold your peace! If you are really struggling because the designs in front of you are just not clicking, it could be time to revisit the brief and in particular the material covered in chapters 3 and 4.

Also, depending on your agreement with your graphic designer, don't be afraid of ditching them and looking for someone else. A lot of clients forget that they are the buyers here. You have a choice over what it is you are buying. When you buy branding, you are buying an asset. Stay in control of where you buy that asset from.

In the case of Broadway Barn, the client liked the direction the project was going in but felt we hadn't quite nailed her brand essence.

So we revisited it together and came up with this route:

The concept, which the client eventually articulated herself during a marathon late night conversation with my partner Holly, uses the feather device representing soft down pillows and total relaxation.

But there is a lovely element at play here that gives the branding a subtle edge, which is that the feather also alludes to the feathers of the chickens she raises to provide fresh eggs at breakfast for her guests at Broadway Barn and that it is, in fact a barn that they are staying in. This slight pull towards the heritage of

Broadway Barn gives the branding that extra depth and intrigue and tells a story.

In hindsight, perhaps we hadn't tightened our grip enough on the essence of Broadway Barn – luxurious relaxation with that twist of character provided by the owner's unique wit and charming personality – before proceeding with the initial concepts.

In the cases of Storm DJs and Chiki Tea, we managed to nail the concept straight away and so there was a minimum amount of decisions to be made by the clients.

The important thing is that you are sure about proceeding to the next step.

STEP 5

The designer presents full designs of the logo, website and business card, using dummy copy (Lorem ipsum)

Once your decision has been made, the graphic designer will take the concept and implement it across the logo, website and business card.

By the end of this stage, you will see each component pretty much exactly how it will appear in the real world.

See opposite for how the Chiki Tea branding works across the logo, website and business card at this stage.

In this case, an illustrator was used for the main imagery. In the case of Broadway Barn a photographer was commissioned for the photography. In both cases this cost extra money to produce but was necessary to elevate the branding to the required standard.

It is during this phase that you have to be vigilant about your budget for extra imagery and let your designer know your limits. During the briefing phase (under "An overview of what is needed") I mentioned the importance of requesting at least several concepts that require minimal if any additional imagery.

It's fair to say though, that you are bound to require some form of additional imagery eventually. With Storm DJs, the "seretonin" graphic device was enough to carry the concept across the business card, but stock imagery was still used for their presentation document and eventually the website.

With regard to the website, brochures and other materials that require chunks of copy, graphic designers

Eight steps to getting branded

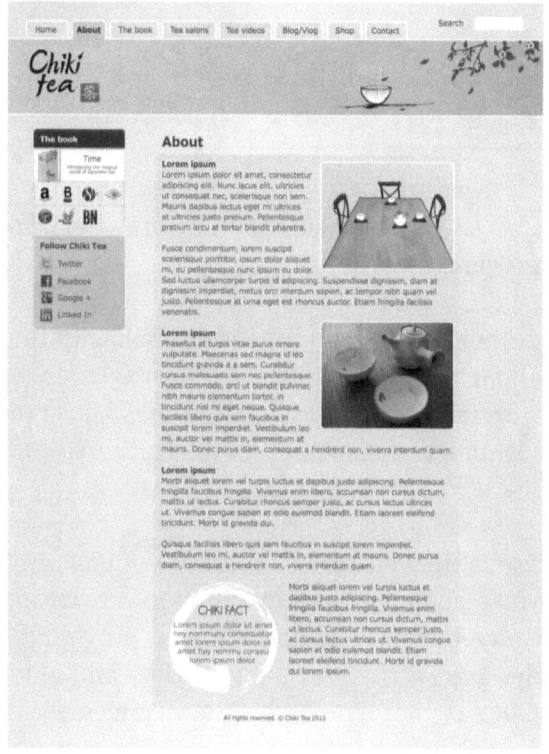

often use placeholder text in the form of latin prose (Lorem ipsum) during this Step. This is dummy copy and aids in giving you an idea of what the designs will look like but also how much content you will need to supply for artworking and production. The word count is vital and your designer will let you know how much room there is to play with.

STEP 6
You submit final content for the website and business card

This step sometimes comes before or even during the previous Step.

Certainly, it is good practice to talk with the designer about the content of the website before they start working into the designs. You really need to sit down together and map out the information that needs to be there.

As mentioned, Lorem ipsum or dummy copy, will give you a good idea of how the finished website is going to look. Now, it is up to you to provide the graphic designer with all of the real copy and other content (such as photography, diagrams, tables, etc.) they need to flow into the website as well as the contact details they need to put on your business card.

It is good practice to have all the information proofread and up to scratch before submitting it, although late changes are often inevitable.

STEP 7
You sign off the designs and the designer puts the project into artwork and production

Once all of your real content has been flowed into the website and business card, it's time for you to press the "Go" button by signing everything off. NO corrections to the printed material can be made beyond this point (although you can always make changes to the electronic files for future prints after this particular print run). The next time you see these components, it'll be in the flesh, you'll have the real items in your hands and the real website up and running.

One of the terms used in the graphic design and branding world is "artwork". Artworking is carried out at the end of a project to ensure that the electronic files are formatted correctly in order to produce the required branding. There is a big difference between designing the various components and the production of them.

The level of artwork required will vary from project to project and branded element to branded element.

During Step 3 (the concepts stage) and sometimes even into the design development stage (Step 5), the graphic designer will use previews of say the logo or any other imagery in order to save time and energy.

So for instance, a logo pre-artwork (below left) is used to convey what the graphic designer sees as your branding during the initial stages of the project. During artwork, the logo is polished, refined and elevated to a professional looking standard (below right).

LOGO   LOGO

This is what the "Chiki" in Chiki Tea looked like during step 1 (below left) and after step 7 (below right):

In the case of a sales brochure, business cards and other printed elements, there will be specific requirements from the printer that the graphic designer must respect in order to avoid anomalies in the production such as colours coming out in a strange hue, or photographs appearing fuzzy and pixillated, or fonts distorting, etc.

For instance, a business card and a brochure will need to be set up specifically for the printer so that the colour bleeds off the edges of the pages properly and so that the folds occur at the right places.

Although this is very much the graphic designer's responsibility, it is worth knowing about. Always feel free to ask the designer whether a detail in the logo that has been bugging you can be or should be tweaked during the artworking phase.

In medium to large sized branding agencies, artworkers and designers occupy separate job roles. The designers will be in charge of the concept generation and the design development, and the artworkers will be in charge of the artwork and production. All of the branding you see around you on billboards, supermarket shelves and magazines has been artworked to a very high specification.

A special mention for website production
It can be confusing for clients to understand the difference between website design and website production. I have seen clients left abandoned with the visuals for a website in PDF format, without understanding that they then have to go and source someone to build the website for them.

A website needs to be designed to work with the other branded elements such as the sales brochure and the business card. It then needs to be built so that it works as a real life, fully-functional website uploaded onto the internet so that people can access it.

When you commission a graphic designer to work on your branding, make sure you know what you are getting. Are you just getting the designs for the website? Or are you also getting the build? It might be the designer who does the build too, or it might be that they work with a web developer to deliver the site with a minimal amount of fuss on your behalf.

Check with your designer to see how much they are prepared to coordinate the production of the site as well as the arrangement of your url, email addresses, website hosting, etc.

Eight steps to getting branded

In the pictures above, you can see what the Chiki Tea homepage looked like during the design phase of the project (left) and after the build (right) by a company called SO Technology. See their website here: **www.sotechnology.co.uk**

STEP 8
Handover meeting between you and the graphic designer

Have your graphic designer arrange for your business cards (and whatever other printed material you have commissioned) to be delivered to your address.

You are now "live"! Your website is up and running and your business cards are in your hands. You have a (mini) brand for your business.

You now have to ensure that you are on top of everything going forwards. That "living entity" as Eisner calls it, your brand, just like your home, needs a certain amount of up-keep.

Your graphic designer should offer you a handover meeting or at the least a Skype call to ensure that you or someone on your team is comfortable managing the brand from here on out.

The meeting should include:

- The graphic designer handing over the electronic files of the logo (screen and print versions) and the business card. These can be on a CD or a USB stick or even by email or Dropbox, etc. This is so that you can get more copies printed later on and also allows you to go to a different graphic designer for other projects for your branding, whatever that might be (an exhibition banner, DVD packaging, posters, merchandise, etc.) if you so choose.

- The graphic designer showing you how to log into your website's admin in order to upload and update content. Usually they will provide you with a short user guide for this.

- Any further questions from you about anything to do with your branding.

At Ashford Perkins, we also tend to include a short "brand guideline" document that shows you what fonts have been used, colour values, use of imagery, use of logo, etc. This is great for your own personal use if, for instance, you want to put a PowerPoint presentation together and would like to know what fonts and colours to use to keep that consistency across the board. It also serves other graphic designers that you may employ further down the line as you create more touch points for your brand.

BONUS STEP
Follow up call with the graphic designer

This tends to be more of a courtesy call than anything else, but it's a great way for the designer to make sure you're happy with everything once a month or two has passed since the handover meeting.

It can also be an opportunity for you to give feedback to the designer and appraise the project so that they can improve their own business practice.

KEY POINTS

- The strategic conversation(s) comes first for a reason. Determine whether you need to commission the project in the first place. Determine what you need out of it and make sure you know what your brand essence is.

- As a repeat from the previous chapter: feed your graphic designer's head with quality content.

- Open communication between you and the graphic designer is key. Always be aware of what stage of the project you are at.

- After the initial concepts stage (step 3), you will have a very good idea about whether this is the right designer for you to finish off your project. Trust your gut. If you don't think it will work, sever the relationship and look for another.

- Brace yourself for the excitement by the end of the process of having a fully-fledged, cohesive and well-designed (mini) branded presence in the market – nothing can beat this feeling as a business owner!

FINAL THOUGHTS

THE TRUTH SHALL PREVAIL

As money flows through markets looking for products and services to latch on to, being invisible as a business holds little merit. A brand crystallises a business's true value into an identifiable interface that market forces can react to.

All of this branding bravado can get people carried away with the endless potential of creating a heightened perception of the value of their business. But this book is not about conning people into buying stuff they don't need. Branding is not about creating a false sense of value.

There is something important to remember. Your logo, website and everything else are delivery systems for a promise that you make to people.

Having read this book and applied the principles, your branding will probably now look incredible (!). You might be promising a lot to your audience through it so make sure you over deliver on that promise through your product. Make sure you exceed all expectations.

There is probably no greater a destroyer of a brand than a product that fails to deliver what it promised to the buyer.

FINAL THOUGHTS

You deliver a more powerful experience to your customers when you under promise and over deliver. Allow your product to be the hero of your branding – let it do the magic. And let the rest of your brand be the messenger that informs people of the potential, but no more.

And therein lies the challenge: create branding that communicates your true value whilst avoiding the spin. Your branding needs to be captivating enough to engage an audience without leading them down the garden path.

Communication between people and businesses takes place at light speed. We live in an era where nearly everything is accessible, all of the time. There is little that can be hidden from those willing to search out the truth. And nor should you feel that you need to hide anything. Brand essence correlates directly with your own personal truth as a business owner, and as a person. Use honesty as your secret weapon. Get as authentic as you can with yourself and others about what you want to create, about what your business is all about.

There is an old Japanese saying that goes: "right heart, right path". If your intention is good, what you manifest from that point outwards will be good accordingly.

Don't worry about your expression (your path) until you identify and speak from your essence (your heart). Once you have your essence defined, your expression will flow effortlessly.

A HIDDEN CODE

Alan Turing (1912 – 1954) was a British mathematician, logician, cryptoanalyst and computer scientist. In 1936 Turing's paper "On Computable Numbers, with an Application to the Entscheidungsproblem" (!) was published. The work is considered among experts as seminal.

In it, Turing was trying to tackle a deeply abstract mathematical problem and in doing so, almost inadvertently, laid the foundation for what became the modern computer.

It was Claude Shannon (1916–2001), an American mathematician, electronic engineer, and cryptographer known as "The father of Information Theory", who picked up from where Turing left off. Shannon took information theory beyond its known constraints at the time and gave information its own unit of measurement. He showed that any message could be translated into binary digits. This had profound consequences on how we can now manipulate, convert and harness information.

In his 1948 paper "A mathematical theory of communication", Shannon explains how information can be broken down into tiny building blocks that make up a message. These building blocks, or "bits" as he christened them, are akin to electrons in that they are fundamental. Post-Shannon, *anything* could be transcribed into binary code, made up of 1's and 0's.

I often like to think of brand essence as the binary code that writes the story of how a brand needs to express itself in order to adapt to market conditions.

The market can be a rough and tumble landscape for businesses of any kind and size. But the further you drill down through its fabric, the deeper you delve into the consciousness of your target audience, the more you understand what drives them, what problems they need to solve and most importantly, how best you can serve them.

Ultimately, your brand essence lies in how you serve your customers, not by giving them what they think they want or need, but how you solve their *problems*, whether they are conscious of them or not.

FINAL THOUGHTS

Written deep in the code of your audience's behaviour, well beneath the surface of the commercial terrain, your brand essence is waiting to be deciphered for the benefit of your brand, for your business and for your customers.

Let the exploration commence!

BRAND ESSENCE EXERCISES

Grab a new notebook and dedicate it to your brand. This will be your brainstorming and researching tool as you think about how you serve your customers, what your brand essence is and how your brand story could unfold.

If you go through these exercises in order, you may feel there is a certain amount of repetition. This will be because each exercise is designed to look at the same problem from a different perspective and so there is bound to be some overlaps. In fact, it could be in these very overlaps where your brand essence lies.

EXERCISE 1
A QUESTION OF IMPORTANCE

Answer this question:

What is the most important thing to your customer?

As you go through the remaining exercises revisit this question and see how your answer morphs as you gain deeper insights.

BRAND ESSENCE EXERCISES

EXERCISE 2
YOUR REAL PRODUCT

In your notebook, write the title PRODUCT at the top. Now read through the entire exercise and then go back and answer the following questions:

- What do you really sell?

- Is it the product you think you sell, or does it go deeper than that?

- Ask other people, preferably your customers or potential customers, what they think it is you really sell.

- Ask these same people what they get out of buying your product. This will help you understand what the real value is that you bring to your customers.

For instance:

- You might sell drills and picture hooks, but what you're really selling is a beautiful picture hanging on someone's bedside wall.

- Storm DJs rents out DJs and DJ equipment, but what

they really sell is happy guests at private parties and events. What host wouldn't want that?

- Chiki Tea sells Japanese tea and educational programmes, but what they really sell is a slice of Japan – a magical journey into a mystical and enchanting wonderland.

EXERCISE 3
THE 100 BENEFITS AND THEIR TOP THREE PROBLEMS

Most people in marketing know about "benefits" and "features". The theory goes that as a business, you are always meant to market your product by focusing not on the features of it but on the benefits it provides to your customer.

For instance, if I were to try to sell you a spade, I wouldn't focus on the fact that it has a special film around the handle (feature) but that as a consequence you can use the spade in all kinds of weather and it wouldn't slip out of your hand (benefit).

This thinking is still OK, valid even, but looks outdated in today's age, especially when whole industries are enjoying a huge amount of success by specifically promoting features (the technology industry in particular).

Bring out your notebook again and make sure you have several clean pages. Write numbers from 1 to 100 down the pages with enough room to write a sentence (one number per line).

Now, write down a list of the *100* benefits your customers get from buying your product. You have to get 100 and I know you can do it! These can be secondary benefits and even further associated benefits. Get into your customers' world and experience how your product has changed it. See things from their side. And make this fun!

Once you have your list, now identify the common theme or thread that runs through it. Use a pen to circle similarities so you can "mine the heart" out of this list.

As you do this, delve deeper into the consciousness of your customer. What's underlying his or her desires, needs and wants. At the route of every single benefit your customer sees in your product is a **problem** that you are solving for them through it. The problems are where the real juice is to be found.

See if you can list three *problems* (not desires or whims or wants) that your customers have. Identify these as your customers' top three "problem sets" that your business works towards solving.

EXERCISE 4
SIMON SAYS

Simon Sinek is the grand master of "why". He is considered the leading authority on what motivates people into action. Sinek has written a book called "Start with Why" which claims to have identified the key to what makes a person or an organization extraordinary.

Sinek observes that every company or person will be able to tell you what they do. Most will be able to tell you how they do it. But it is only the rare, true legends remembered throughout history, who can tell you *why* they do what they do or did what they did.

It is this *why* that Sinek has identified as the fuel for making a person or an organization of any sort, stand out from the rest over time.

BRAND ESSENCE EXERCISES

I would argue that we associate really great brands with organizations that express their purpose, their essence, their heart or their *why* in the most succinct and honest manner.

To achieve this they are extremely clear on what it is they want to say about themselves – what it is they want to share with their audience. Great brands speak from the heart directly to the hearts of their customers.

In this simple exercise, watch Simon Sinek's TED Talk by visiting his website: **www.startwithwhy.com**

After watching this 18 minute inspiring talk, get your notebook out and answer the following questions:

- ***Why* does your business exist?**

- ***Why* is your business valuable to your customers?**

- ***Why* do your customers need your product?**

These are often personal questions for business owners. When you have them answered, you will shake your world and the world of those you want to affect.

EXERCISE 5
IDENTIFY YOUR TARGET AUDIENCE

In writing this book I wanted to place a huge emphasis on finding your brand essence.

But it would be a disservice not to bring up the importance of identifying your target audience. Uncovering your true value and articulating the heart of your business goes hand-in-hand with identifying who your target audience is. As you will have seen in exercise 3, by thinking about the problems you solve for people, you are simultaneously establishing who has those problems to begin with.

Make sure your graphic designer knows how your audience likes to communicate. How do they naturally interact with their friends, family and with the organizations they are already doing business with? Your designer needs to be sensitive to what these people **value** most in their lives.

Be aware of the language they feel most comfortable using – turns of phrase, visual cues, interests, points of reference, etc.

Start with a clean sheet of paper in your notebook. We

are now going to put you in your customers' shoes!

- Who does your product help?

- What do they look like?

- How do they behave?

- What's important to them?

- Where do they work?

- What are their hobbies?

- What age and ethnicity?

- Do they tweet, pin and flickr? Or do they dial, meet and eat?

EXERCISE 7
THE END OF GENDER

Watch the TED Talk by Johanna Blakley called 'Social media and the end of gender':

http://tinyurl.com/7a6bvxf

Johanna Blakley shows us how traditional methods of categorizing demographics have gone completely out the window thanks to the internet. This is because, as she puts it, people are interested in people who are interested in the same things as them. It doesn't matter how old or what country you are from. If you like vanilla ice cream, you want to get to know other vanilla ice cream fans, no matter where they live, how old they are or what kind of car they drive.

It's an interesting angle on the subject of consumer demographics and psychographics and should offer you either a good contrasting perspective or booster to Exercise 4.

EXERCISE 7
TEST DRIVE YOUR BRANDING

> *"I've failed over and over and over again in my life and that is why I succeed."*
> – Michael Jordan

Branding, like anything in business, needs to be market-tested. Sometimes we can spend far too long trying to perfect the look of something only for it to eventually get rejected by the market. The market is the ultimate testing ground for whether we have created something of value or not.

This is not to say we don't have to strive for something that looks good. Commissioning a competent graphic designer with a strong brand essence and brief will set you up nicely. But beware of perfectionism, especially if you are launching something new.

For this exercise, I want you to simply put your branding out there. Chuck it onto the market. Hand out your cards, your brochures, and drive people to your website. Ask for feedback but just listen to it for a while before acting on it. This is the fire, then aim approach. After it's out there for a while or so, see if your branding needs tweaking, then tweak it. If it needs removing, remove it. If it flies, let it fly and steer it.

Remember Eisner's words "a brand is a living entity...". It has to adapt to the market environment or it will die. Through time you will always have to update your branding. Branding is not static, it is a fluid process and needs to change with the times.

Of course the best branding *changes* the times. It dictates what the future looks like. But most branding has to evolve to accommodate new trends, new ways of understanding the world, new visual and technological reference points. As long as you refrain from doing it every week, your logo can be updated, modernized, tweaked, and adapted later if necessary.

HEART-FELT THANKS

A huge, warm thank you to the following people:

My wife Holly Helt; parents Judith and Stewart Sanson; sister Clare Green; brother-in-law Andy Green; and my nieces Layla and Freya; Pa Green and Judy; Jasmine; and the rest of my family on all sides for their unconditional support and love.

Jackie Coe, amongst several others, who agreed to be interviewed, read through the first drafts and gave me invaluable feedback.

Mindi McLean and Adam McGlue for letting me use their businesses as case studies.

John-Paul Bland for letting me use his photography on the web pages of Broadway Barn. www.jpbland.co.uk

Peter J. Thomson and Klaus Bravenboer at Fuel Story for their bow tie model. www.fuelstory.com

Steven Oddy and his team at SO technology for all their work on the Chiki Tea website and for letting me use their website visuals. www.sotechnology.co.uk

Daniel Priestley and Thao Dang at Entrevo as well as everyone within the Key Person of Influence team and community. This wouldn't have happened without you in particular. www.entrevo.com

ABOUT THE AUTHOR

ABOUT THE AUTHOR

Alexander Sanson studied Graphic Design at Norwich School of Art and Design and Bath Spa University College.

After his final year (2002) he headed back to London to secure freelance jobs and apprenticeships at some of the world's most prestigious graphic design and branding agencies including Landor Associates, the Brand Union (Enterprise IG at the time) and Identica. He worked on accounts for Vodafone, Brewsters, Philips, Volvo, Seat and Russian Standard.

Alexander then went on to work full-time at Williams and Phoa on accounts for Rolls-Royce, WHSmith, Allied Domecq and EADS.

Two years later he moved over to the design team at global PR agency Hill & Knowlton, working on accounts for Allianz, HSBC, Carling, and adidas.

In 2007 Alexander went freelance, working on-site at branding studios for clients such as Barclays, KPMG, Visa and Tesco as well as consulting independently with a number of small businesses.

In 2010, he co-founded Ashford Perkins, specialising in helping small businesses address their needs by using branding more effectively.

ABOUT THE AUTHOR

Praise for Alexander Sanson

"Alexander, right from the outset of his phase 1 audit meeting, surveying my business laid out on the ground, was able to define in words the vision I have for my company. Very quickly he was able to construct a clear path for how my ideas could become products, setting out a journey progressing through key stages in my brand development. His enthusiasm was inspiring, taking the thought process to much higher levels. I left with a clear plan and drive that in weeks I have been able apply to make my brand stronger ... If you are running every aspect of your business like me then Alexander is worth his weight in Gold. I have been very fortunate to bump into him."
– Rollo Mahon, Corenergy and the Barefoot Academy

"Alex played a key role in launching a global movement with their work on the Beers for Books logos. The logos have been used to promote events on 4 continents and have given us a visual identity that perfectly matches our mission and the branding we aim to achieve."
– Gary Bremermann, Beers for Books

ABOUT THE AUTHOR

"Alex is extraordinarily talented, creative and customer-oriented. He listened carefully to our mission, aspirations, and budget and developed a fun and engaging concept for the event we were planning and fabulous materials to support it. The invitations captivated everyone's curiosity. We had a wonderful turnout for our evening and everyone was ready to celebrate thanks to the tone and energy set by the invite and related materials. We will definitely call on Alex for future occasions."
– Cathy Pike, TELL

"Effective branding, which starts with the right logo and follows through to all forms of communication, requires strategic thinking and attention to detail. Alex is excellent at providing the whole package."
– Mindi McLean, Broadway Barn

www.ingramcontent.com/pod-product-compliance
Lightning Source LLC
Chambersburg PA
CBHW030748180526
45163CB00003B/946